THE 5 GREATEST
DISAPPOINTMENTS
IN
HEAVEN

Lynn DePeal

ISBN 978-1-64300-169-2 (Paperback)
ISBN 978-1-64300-170-8 (Digital)

Covenant Books, Inc.
11661 Hwy 707
Murrells Inlet, SC 29576
www.covenantbooks.com

INTRODUCTION

There has been a lot spoken and written about heaven since the beginning of time. Just about everyone has an opinion of what it is going to be like and what we will do there. Some think we will be like angels floating on clouds; others believe we will spend eternity playing harps and singing with saints of old praises to God. A lot is said about who will and who won't be there. Nearly everyone believes that their picture of heaven is correct. And some have even written that they died, went there, and came back with more information on what to expect. Certainly those who speak about heaven believe it will be a perfect place with no sorrow, pain, or disappointments. So as I write this book, I am concerned that I might make many people angry. Just like the lady at church who, when told about my idea for this book, replied, "There are no disappointments in heaven." I hope she is right, but I am finding it difficult to imagine how every-one will get that wish.

So at the risk of being called a heretic by the faithful, I will plunge into this and give you a glimpse of how my warped mind works. I should give what is considered an apology today. I am sorry if anyone was offended by my writing. In other words, I don't really apologize; I just put the onus on you to change your thinking. I can't be blamed for the way God created my brain. If you don't like it, that's your problem, not mine. You will see that this is not a theo-logical treatise. Just the ramblings of my distorted mind that probably needs an electric shock treatment

PROLOGUE

I have to warn you that I sometimes get accused of having a screw loose somewhere in my confused brain. My thinking is reportedly somewhat obscure and convoluted. A common comment from others when I enter into a conversation is, "What in the world are you talking about?" My wife tells me frequently that I am wasting my time and energy worrying about things that will probably never happen and are certainly crazy trivial thoughts. I have to admit that she is probably right. I may have a slight tendency to let my mind wander away from the topic at hand and lose track of the subject being discussed. My mind meanders to another place and time and often arrives somewhere that no one else considers relevant. Sometimes I just blurt out a topic that baffles everyone because it seemingly has no tie to the topic being discussed. But they are mistaken. Somewhere in the conversation, there is a link to what I am saying. There is always a link. My comment, joke, story, or anecdote always make perfect sense to me. Somewhere in the distant recesses of my mind, I have made a connection. The electrical impulses and synapses in my brain have simply taken a less-than-traveled route to a place buried deep in my memory. But my memories are not shared by others in the same way they are to me. The puzzled looks on others' faces simply mean that they have not kept up with what I am thinking. Believe me, there is path from my off-the-wall comment to an important event that may be decades old but still fresh on my jogged memory.

It was one of these experiences that has led me to writing this book. The book idea was conceived a long time ago in 2001. I had married my near-perfect wife in 1997, who by the way had University of Michigan season football tickets. My son had asked Nancy how long it was after I found out about the season tickets that I asked her to marry me. She said about thirty minutes. I guess she wasn't so perfect since it was actually nineteen minutes. In 1997, Michigan had completed a perfect regular season and would be going to the Rose Bowl to play the Washington State University Cougars and their highly touted quarterback Ryan Leaf. A victory by Michigan would likely lead to a National championship. We couldn't go to that game but it put a dream in our heads to go to a Rose Bowl game in the future.

So back to 2001, Michigan again was going to the Rose Bowl; and this time, we were going to the game. But we had a cat and had the issue of what to do with it. A cat that I didn't like but had inherited from my wife's daughter, who couldn't keep him because her roommate simply didn't like cats. I informed my wife that her roommate didn't like cats either. She thought that was a weak excuse. I tried to conjure up a severe allergy, but all I could come up with is that I hated cats. Not good enough. So we had the cat and now had the dilemma of what to do with her (or did I say him before?) since you never can tell about cats; even the vet got confused.

So in the midst of discussing what to do about the cat while we went to the football game in Pasadena, I had the idea for a book. I believe I said something like this as we were telling friends about the Rose Bowl trip. I need to write a book called *The Five Greatest Disappointments in Heaven*.

Everyone looked at me as if I were crazy. "What does that have to do with the Rose Bowl?"

"It makes perfect sense to me," I replied.

Going to the Rose Bowl, what about the cat?, Rose Bowl, 1966, what will heaven be like? Can't you just see the connection? It's all clear in my mind. While everyone scratched their heads trying to figure out my logical connections, I started the process of laying out the introduction and the organization of the chapters.

CHAPTER 1

I have loved football ever since I can remember. I had dreams of being a great football player, and of course, I would be a great quarterback. But the lack of the right genes and the lack of determination to build my 5'10, 140-pound body into a chiseled specimen severely dampened my dreams. Of course, what I lacked in physique, I also lacked in speed. Running a 6.8 second forty yard dash for a skinny, no-muscle athlete usually means the end of a dream. So my football participation came to an end as a junior in high school when the revelation came that football was not a good career path. But I still loved the game.

I used to walk a mile and half to Waldo Stadium and watch Western Michigan University Broncos practice. Sometimes I would get to pay a dollar and watch a real game. In 1961, I even got to watch a top team in Utah State Aggies come to Waldo Stadium to play Western

Michigan. I saw one of the greats, Merlin Olsen, and a young quarterback Bill Munson play that day. What a thrill for a young teenager to watch some awesome football. I will never forget the many kickoff returns or touchdowns that day. Western got smoked that day, but they did score 22 points. Only Baylor scored more points against Utah State that year when they beat the Aggies in the Gotham Bowl 24–9.

In 1965, I graduated from Kalamazoo Central High School and went off to college at a little known Christian College named Owosso College. It was located thirty-five miles northeast of Lansing, Michigan, the home of the Michigan State University Spartans. My roommate happened to be huge State fan and kept trying to convince me how great the Spartans were. He kept bugging me to go to a game. I had always been a Michigan Wolverine fan because I liked the helmets. And when my friend and fellow football player from junior high and high school, Ron Thompson, went to Ann Arbor, Michigan, because he was a great high school player, I was totally sold on Michigan. Our football careers had parted in high school because of my weak, spindly body and his 6'1, 210-pound athletic frame.

So why would I go with my roommate to watch Moo Tech play when I aligned myself with the far superior university and nationally renowned football team. After all, the Wolverines had gone 9–1 in 1964 and were getting back their championship groove. But my roommate persisted and finally I agreed to go to a game. Skeptical and snooty (aren't all Michigan fans), I decided to appease him and go watch the Sparties. With snide comments about their cheerleaders grazing on the sidelines, we headed off to Spartan Stadium with our dollar student tickets in hand. But of course we weren't going to sit in the student section. My roommate's dad was a ramp guard on the Spartan fifty-yard line. We only had to move five or six times before no one kicked us out of their seats. And his dad wasn't going to escort us to the gate.

So we settled in to watch my first Big Ten Football game. October 2, 1965, the Michigan Spartans vs. the Illinois Fighting Illini. Of course, they were without the greatest linebacker of all time, Dick Butkus, who had gone on to play for the Chicago Bears, but they still were led by a top running back named Jim Grabowski. The Spartans had gotten off to a pretty good start with wins over UCLA

Bruins and Penn State Nittany Lions, but my Wolverines were also 2–0 and were playing Georgia while I was sitting at Spartan Stadium. I didn't expect much from the Green and White, and I was sure that Michigan would be 3–0 when they played state the following week. As I sat in the stadium that day, something changed within me. A whole new cast of characters opened up before me and the contagion of my friends' enthusiasm got the best of me and I opened my mind to new possibilities. I was watching a special team with special players. Guys like Bubba Smith, George Webster, Steve Juday, Clinton Jones, Gene Washington, and Bob Apisa. Wow, these guys were good, and I was actually there watching something special unfold before me. My Wolverines were being replaced by something real. I was a fan. Go Green-Go White.

State beat Illinois that day and Michigan lost to Georgia, so the showdown in Ann Arbor lost some of its luster and after the Wolverines got trounced by the Spartans. The now shifted expectations looked to the future for a possible Rose Bowl rematch with UCLA.

And the dream became reality. Michigan State swept the Big Ten and UCLA won the PAC-10. The traditional showdown would take place at the Rose Bowl in Pasadena on January 1, 1966. The granddaddy of them all. A win by the Spartans would cement their position as National Champions. No Disputes, No Controversy. All they had to do was beat the Bruins before a national audience, but it was not to be. Led by Gary Beban, UCLA edged out the Spartans 14–12 to avenge the season opener loss to State. Fumbles, mistakes, and penalties ended the hope for an undefeated season and that unchallenged national championship. The dream had ended.

No, the dream had just begun. I was a fan. The main players would be back. No early leaving for the NFL back then. No one knew about those Spartans in 1965, but now it was 1966 and the future was bright. The team would be ready. No setbacks this year. A fan's dream. Hurry up, September, this would be the year.

The season began on September 17, 1966. The Spartans were ranked number 2 in the pre-season poll but that would change quickly after knocking off a pretty good North Carolina State team. Now number 1 and facing Penn State, they solidified their ranking by trouncing the Nittany Lions 42–8. Yes, this was the year. Now a victory over Illinois in Champaign, Illinois, and a solid win over that forgotten team from Ann Arbor clearly showed that the number 1 ranking was no fluke.

But a less-than-awesome win over a mediocre Ohio State team bumped the Spartans back to number 2. Who could possibly move them from the top spot? Notre Dame. The media's love child. After State's lackluster performance at Ohio State and Notre Dame's impressive trouncing of perennial power Oklahoma, the drop was inevitable. But the world would be righted when the Spartans and Notre Dame would meet in November. Back to business, the Spartans cruised past an excellent Purdue team 41–20 who, by the way, went to and won the Rose Bowl since Michigan State could not go two years in a row.

Victories over Northwestern, Iowa, and Indiana set the stage for the greatest game of the century. Number 1 Notre Dame vs. number 2 Michigan State. The storied program vs the Dream Team.

I really didn't know much about Notre Dame except the stories I had heard at Big Joe Wright's barber shop in Kalamazoo, Michigan. Big Joe was a local celebrity sports announcer in Kalamazoo and lots of sports guys came to his shop. I even saw Charlie "Old Paw Paw" Maxwell, "Mr. Sunday," home-run guy for the Detroit Tigers in the '60s, getting his haircut one day. Lots of those guys were Notre Dame fans, and I heard that school mentioned a lot. I had heard stories about the Fighting Irish from legendary coaches to miracles wins. It seemed to me that Notre Dame got a lot of attention from the media and often got preference when picking National Champions. I had even heard about Touchdown Jesus at the stadium. But I was a Protestant and I had been taught to distrust those Catholics. Their idea that God was on their side was a myth. God loved the underdog and the hodgepodge team at Michigan State with cast-off Black players from the South mixed with White players from the Midwest were certainly underdogs. Michigan State even tossed in a barefoot kicker from Hawaii named Dick Kenney. The Spartans practiced diversity before it even had a name.

And I was a Spartan fan now and this was the game. History and legends no longer mattered. The Spartans would not falter now. This game would prove that they were not upstarts. They were the real champions and rightly deserved number 1.

I actually remember little about that game. The only recollections were that I couldn't get into the game even with my roommate's Dad being a ramp guard. The game was a sellout and the largest attendance in Spartan Stadium until being surpassed in 1990 when state again hosted Notre Dame. I also recall that Michigan State scored first and looked like they might take complete control. But Notre Dame, even without their starting quarterback Terry Hanratty who had to leave the game after a big hit by Bubba Smith in the first Quarter, fought back and kept the game close. The Fighting Irish were also missing Nick Eddy, the Heisman candidate, because he slipped and fell on the ice getting off the bus in East Lansing. So Notre Dame had every reason to make excuses for not being their best. And of course Notre Dame fans did whine that they would have dominated if their superstars were playing. But the game was deadlocked at 10–10.

A missed field goal and an under thrown ball to a wide open, Gene Washington finally brought the game down to a Spartan punt and Notre Dame first and 10 from their own 30. Still tied, everyone in the stands at Spartan Stadium and those listening at home figured that the Hall of Fame coach Ara Parsegian would prove to everyone that his team was a true champion and would give it their all to win one for the Gipper. Another Notre Dame miracle was certainly going to happen. But no, Ara decided to tie one for the Gipper;. He ran out the clock. In today's game, he probably would have taken a knee. No chances. No trick plays. No Hail Marys. Just play for a tie.

Everyone knows that a true champion never quits, never gives up, and plays it right to the end. So when the media gave the National Championship to Notre Dame, I made a lifetime vow. I would always hate Notre Dame. I would always mock their legendary coach. Fifty years later, people still tell me to let it go. No one should carry bitterness and anger for so long. But I won't let it go, my grudge is to be held forever.

Somehow, I have moved on from the Michigan State Spartans. My roommate transferred to Michigan State and became a doctor. I moved on, got married, and had kids. Coincidentally, I married Ron Thompson's cousin, so my former friend and all-American high school football player was now my cousin by marriage. Ron's football career didn't work out so well at Michigan so he changed career paths and became a dentist.

My marriage didn't work out so well and I guess Ron is no longer my cousin.

So twenty years ago, I met and married the greatest woman I had ever known. She was cute, sweet, kind, and unbelievably upbeat, and she was a Michigan grad with season tickets. My fan loyalty switched completely. Michigan won the National championship a month after we got married and I was now a Wolverine by marriage. I got to bathe in the glory of The Victors, champions of the West; the winningest football program of all time and; the Leaders and Best. I even got to brag about my Wolverines even to the point of letting some new friends from Nebraska know that when Tom Osborne (who claimed a share of the 1997 national championship) got to heaven, he would find that the most magnificent mansion in heaven was adorned in everything Michigan. When Tom complained that Lloyd Carr shouldn't get rewarded more than him since they had shared the championship, Saintt Peter pointed out the Mansion was not Lloyd's but God's.

I was an all-in fan. We had season tickets, four seats, and every home game now. Nancy and I, plus two friends or family, at Michigan Stadium. Section 13, row 59, seats 5–8, right behind the flag pole, but we were there—cheering, screaming, berating Refs—being a fan.

I loved it and thank goodness, so did my wife. A perfect fit. A great new life. No more disappointments.

That led to our trip to the Rose Bowl on January 1, 2002, and how I got to thinking about this book. The segues in my mind are perfectly clear. But not everyone can quite get the connections, so I'll explain again.

We were planning a trip to the Rose Bowl. We had to find a solution for the cat. Did I say how much I hated cats?. What do I possibly hate more than cats? Just one thing: Notre Dame. Top of the list, even more than Ohio State. So the only solution to my bitterness will be to die and go to heaven where there will be no disappointments. But maybe, just maybe, when I get there, I will suffer one of the greatest disappointments of all. I may find out that in the end

Jesus really is a Notre Dame fan.

CHAPTER 2

I think it safe to say that nearly everyone loves kittens. Cute, adorable, cuddly, lovable kittens. The penalty for saying anything bad about a kitten would bring calls for the death penalty, or at least complete expulsion from society. Complete isolation with no thought of friendship or human companionship. But there is a problem with the idyllic picture. Those kittens grow up to be cats, and now this consensus turns quickly to division and conflict. To say it mildly, not everyone loves cats. For those who are not fond of cats, the spectrum ranges from dislike to absolute hatred. For those who enjoy cats there is not much of a range. On that side it is complete affection and love. So it was when I married Nancy. I was informed "love me–love my cat." Now, I loved Nancy, but I couldn't quite pull off the "love my cat" thing. Those of you that despise cats can understand my dilemma. It is nearly impossible to move from the extreme position of cat-hater to cat-tolerance.

The cat was actually my wife's daughter, Sarah's, cat. Nancy was keeping it for Sarah since she was away at college living with several girls, one of which didn't like cats. But Sarah only had one more year of school and maybe then she would get a place of her own and could take the cat. Just one year. I guess I could put up with this creature for a year. So graduation came and wouldn't you know it, Sarah moved into a new apartment and shared it with all her old roommates. We still had the cat. Hope for reuniting the cat with its rightful owner were fading. But times change in young women's lives so a short time later the "I don't like cats" roommate got engaged to the man of her dreams and moved away with her fiancé. Sarah got a place of her own, now was the time, the cat would certainly go now. And the move was made but wait, it was not to be. Sarah had met a great young man in Chicago. This could be the one. I was very happy for her because he was perfect for her. Almost. He had one major flaw—he was allergic to cats. He couldn't come to her place without suffering severe allergic reactions. There was no way she was going to jeopardize this relationship for a cat. So the cat came back. We thought it was a gone but the cat came back. Forever with us, not with her rightful owner. Sarah even warned her newfound love that if he broke up with her, she would fill his car with cat hair.

So here I am, with a cat I despise. I had been able to tolerate this living arrangement with the hope that there was a promising end point, but now the future looked very bleak. Life forever with a cat, what could be more depressing?

This was not an old cat. Probably was on number two or three of its nine lives. There had to be a solution. Maybe the cat would "run away," or it would it would fall into a deep depression and throw itself in front of a truck. No such luck. I was doomed to live my life with this pathetic worthless creature, and this cat had no redeeming qualities. I do have to concede that some cats actually provide some sort of warped companionship and unhealthy comfort to their owners. For some, cats are their closest friend or like a child to them, but this was not the case for me. I detested that cat.

The cat was named Haley. My wife had gotten the cat for her daughter years before we met. The cat was identified as a beautiful all-white longhaired girl; therefore the name Haley. Adorable little kitten, but as I said before, that perfect kitten began to grow into a cat and the flaws began to appear. The cat was deaf as are many all-white, blue-eyed felines. The cat was not warm and cuddly but arrogant, distant, and stubborn. The cat wasn't even a girl. When my wife took the cat to the vet to get neutered, he actually started the female surgery only to discover Haley was a male. But the name was there so Haley it was. I do understand the bit about being saddled with a girl's name. Whatever gave my mother the idea that Lynn was a good name for a boy. I did think it was a pretty good idea when I was put in the girl's gym class in the eighth grade. What teenage boy has not had that dream? That interjection into the story almost took me down a different memory lane, but fortunately I forced myself back to the story at hand. Not sure where I would have ended up with that memory circling my brain.

Not even our dog liked the cat. I couldn't tell for sure if he hated him but he seemed to tolerate her just as I did, at least for a while. Haley was always eating the dog food, attacking him while he slept, and generally being a nuisance and bother to this terrific canine. He would put up with it for just so long and then grab the cat, and drag her over to a corner, and drop her there. He roughed her up just enough to let know that he meant business. There I go, calling the cat a her. I can't quite get that out of my mind. We should have changed the name. Just like me, the dog would never hurt Haley. I don't ever understand how anyone can be cruel to a pet, but I have separated my total loathing of the cat from any cruelty.

The world is really split into two camps. Those who love dogs and despise cats and those who love cats and like dogs. It's funny how people who love cats seem to appreciate all animals while dog lovers tend to be one-animal-only people. And of the dog lovers, they either like the big lovable dogs like Golden Retrievers, Labs, or Collies or the little yappy, excitable, pee-on-the-floor dogs that owners think everyone loves. When we spend the winter in Naples, Florida, there are lots of people who bring their little yappers into Publix and put their precious ones on the checkout when they pay for groceries. I could have ended up in prison if I had acted on what I was thinking. You can probably tell which camp I fall into.

So back to my dilemma, what to do with the cat. Sarah did marry the love of her life, the cat-allergic Tim. That option was totally gone so it appeared I was stuck.

There are good reasons not to like cats. In fact, we should all abhor them. We should distance ourselves from them because they are evil devil worshipers. You can see it in their eyes. They are haughty, aloof, sneaky, and certainly not trustworthy. Dogs will go to heaven, I'm certain about that. There is even a movie about dogs that confirms this fact. If it's in a movie, it must be true. But not cats. They will be destined to life forever with their devil master.

You are probably asking, "How in the world can this lovable author have such a disdain for cats? How could someone become so hateful toward my wonderful Fluffy?"

I guess I do owe you an explanation.

I did not always hate cats. In fact, I, just like you, thought kittens were adorable. As a young boy, we had many litters of kittens in our neighborhood. All the kids loved seeing and playing with these new arrivals. Our family never had a cat. We were dog people, and we had a wonderful cocker spaniel pet for most of my early years. When she got hit by a car and died, I cried for days.

So I never grew up with a cats. My only contact was with kittens.

When I was in high school, I had a very interesting teacher, Mrs. Mauzy, who taught the early development of Western Civilization. She introduced me to the history of the Egypt, Greece, and Persia. I became infatuated by the leaders of the Persian Empire notably Xerxes and his son Artaxerxes. When I found out that he had a Persian cat name Xerxes, I wanted one too.

I really didn't know much about cats and I guess I missed some history, but I thought a Persian cat and a Siamese cat were pretty much the same. So I went out and found a Siamese cat and brought it home as my pet. I couldn't name him Xerxes and copy my teacher and Artaxerxes seemed too long, so I named him Plato. So I got a Siamese cat because of my study of Persia and give him a Greek name. Makes a lot of sense to me.

The cat was aloof, haughty, not trainable, and had evil-looking eyes. But I chalked up all these disturbing qualities as freethinking, intelligent, and a stubborn refusal to conform to the herd. All the qualities that I admired and sought to emulate. I was all of these and my cat was just like me. No matter that no one else in the family or circle of friends liked this cat, he was different and that was a good thing.

Then I went off to college and my parents had control of the cat. They saw no redeeming value in the cat and gladly took it to the Humane Society, hoping to unload him on someone else. They tried to convince me that someone would find him enjoyable, but as a near-adult now, I knew that would never happen.

I went without a cat until I married and moved away from my parents. Now I could have a cat again and my wife and I picked up a cute kitten that seemed a perfect fit. And you know, he was a pretty good cat. Slightly arrogant, often aloof, stubborn, and with a mind of its own, he still made a good companion while I was busy with work and school, and my wife's work schedule made for lots of alone time at home.

When our son was born, we had to move to a different apartment and we could not have pets there, so we gave up the cat for our child and moved on. We missed the cat a bit but not enough to get another one. We went several years without a real pet. We tried a couple of shelter dogs but those didn't pan out too well due to our busyness and living circumstances. It was many years later after my twin daughters were around six that I gave in to their begging for a kitten. Who can resist the expectant eyes of your little girls and their pleading for a pet (and I had two of them)? No dad could resist, so off we went to pick up a kitten from some friends who lived on a farm and always seemed to have a new litter available.

The girls loved that cat. They named him Butterscotch, and in their eyes, he could do no wrong. At least I was told it was a him, but I never took a real close look. Just like the vet, I'm not sure I would have known what to look for. Who really knows about cats. The only real proof is when you end up with a litter of kittens. But now I had to live with a cat. No childhood or teenage perceptions to cloud my judgement of what cats were really like. So my attitude slowly began to shift. From excitement in pleasing my daughters, to tolerance of an invader of our home, to dislike for an animal with no redeeming value, to planning ways to get rid of this worthless creature. My opportunity came when I got up one night to find the cat licking some butter we had forgotten to put away and was sitting on the kitchen counter. It also appeared that the cat had mistaken the butter for a litter box. My patience had ended, and over the sad pleadings of my daughters, we took the cat back to the farm for a better life. I don't think my daughters have fully forgiven me for discarding their precious kitty. Now we were cat-less. I was happy. In fact, I was ecstatic. But I had to cover that ecstasy to mourn a bit with my daughters. Yet my thrill only lasted for a while. My girls were grief-stricken by the loss of their beloved Butterscotch. What is a father to do? Everyone knows what happens next. I couldn't bear to see my twins in such pain. No father can be happy when he sees such sadness in his daughters' eyes. So back to the farm for another kitten. We would pick better this time. We would replace the not-so-nice cat with a better one. All would be well. I would tolerate the cat, the girls would smile again. Everything would be just fine. But as John Pinette always proclaimed, "Nay Nay. Nothing is ever fine with a cat." This one turned out to be bipolar. Sweet and lovable at times and a raging demon at others. From kissing and snuggling the family, to a stalking predator at others. Just as God created them to be. Not a pet but a wild killer in the jungle. Mankind should not disturb the natural order of things. Nothing good comes from that interference. So one day when our cousin's son, Paul, got viciously attacked by this wild beast, I grabbed the evil one and tossed him in the trunk for a trip back to the farm. I heard that this creature got into numerous fights with the other cats in my friend's barn and created all kinds of havoc. Not long after that, he was chasing another cat across the road and got hit by a car. I thought it was a deserving end. My cat-loving friends don't like me to talk like that. The truth really hurts.

That would be the end of cats for me. No more need for tolerance. No more attempts at redeeming the little devils. No more pretense that a cute, adorable kitten could turn into a warm friendly cat. The dividing line was clear. Dog lovers had it right. Cat lovers were mentally unbalanced. There was no middle ground.

Many years later, my marriage also ended. It seems that she thought of me the way I thought of cats: life would be better without me. I'm sure she was right.

After my divorce, I went to a singles group at church where there were a lot of cat-loving single ladies. They loved their cats, treated them like people. But I knew better. Hiding behind those whiskers was evil personified. Once when our group was going on a canoe trip on the Pier Marquette River, many of the ladies were concerned about leaving their precious kitties at home. I offered to take care of them on the trip and I assured them the cats would not get wet. No one trusted my offer but when they showed up at the landing, I had a big garbage bag hanging on a tree with a sign that said: Deposit Cats Here. I thought it was a good idea, no one else did. I don't think I was ever fully forgiven for that incredibly great idea. I am still somewhat haunted by the look on Pam Robinson's face when she saw that trash bag. Her look confirmed that she thought I was the cruelest subhuman she had ever met. Ladies, it was just a joke. So these years later, I apologize at the urging of my wife. I am truly sorry that you didn't think it was a joke. My wife still doesn't like that story. She says that it makes people misunderstand what a kind, caring person that I am. Did I tell you how sweet and kind my wife is? I told her that the people who read this book would never be confused about what kind of guy I am. I do hope that any misunderstandings are now cleared up and all those ladies will now think of me with warm memories.

I did meet the love of my life in that singles group and we got married in November of 1997. I sold my condo and we moved into her home in East Grand Rapids. What a great place to live. Wonderful neighbors. Terrific community. We had season tickets to Michigan football, she had a golden retriever, East Grand Rapids had a fabulous high school football team, and remember I told you that she was cute, sweet, kind and unbelievably upbeat. Furthermore, she told her parents, friends, and brothers that I was perfect. I was living the dream. Nothing could be better. Except— she had that cat. It didn't take long for my long-held beliefs about cats to be confirmed.

My wife loves tradition, and holidays are a time to decorate the home with all of the remembrances of Christmas. We have twelve full tubs of Christmas decorations and all of them must be put out in the proper place at Christmas time. So it was no surprise when she got out the handmade nativity scene and place it in the revered place. The reason for the season. The celebration of everything we both believe. The perfect setting. The most prominent place. But not to everyone. The evil, devil cat couldn't stand seeing the baby Jesus in the manger so every time we left the house we came home to find that our daughter's precious cat had swept Jesus out of the manger with his paw. No other figure or decoration was ever touched—just Jesus, swatted away.

The Satan cat thought he had won. But I knew a better day was coming. We were able to pass the cat onto Sarah's brother, Andy, and his roommate, Brendon. It took several years for that cat to go through all of its lives but he finally went on to his eternal destination. I'm positive I know where that is. I was totally shed of that cat and would never have to deal with cats from now through eternity. But you know the physical reality is often taken over by the mental possibility. And you have a glimpse into my mind. I have the constant nagging fear that there will be a second disappointment in heaven.

God has a Cat.

CHAPTER 3

My wife says that I have a great singing voice. She says that she loves to hear me sing. She loves it when I give my short renditions of Elvis or Johnny Cash. I do break out with a couple of lines of "All Shook Up" or "Let Me Be Your Teddy Bear" once in a while. My favorite is "Can't Help Falling in Love," though, and I imagine that I sound just like Elvis when I'm belting it out in the shower. I even end it with, "Thank you, thank you very much." The "Ring of Fire" by Johnny Cash is a close second. But deep down, I know she's lying to me. Remember I told you how sweet and kind she is? She would never want to hurt my feelings or put a damper on my fantasies. I can just see myself, on the big stage, mesmerizing the huge crowd with my fabulous voice. My fans love me and I give them the best I've got. "Encore! Encore! Encore!" Yet, I cannot bring myself to showcase my talents in front of any audience, even to do karaoke. My friend Jerry keeps trying to get me to do it, but I don't want to be embarrassed or find out that everyone (except my wife) was right. It is better to hold on to fantasies than to have them dashed by solid evidence.

I know she's lying to me because I've been told since I was a little boy that I couldn't sing. "Just step away from the real singers so you don't ruin the rendition." "Somebody's off key." "That's not the melody or the harmony." "Oh. It's Lynn. Everyone knows he can't carry a tune."

And so it goes.

I fell in love in the first grade. I remember it so vividly. Traverse Heights Elementary School, Traverse City, Michigan. Ms. Marian. She was beautiful and so sweet and kind. And she certainly loved me too since she was always coming to my desk to make sure I was keeping up. She came to *my desk* more than the other kid's just to smile and say she really loved to see that I was doing my best. Oh, that smile made me feel wonderful inside. I'd do anything for Miss Marian.

So when it came time for the annual school Christmas concert, I was eager to make our class look real good in front of the whole school. Ms. Marian would get a lot of praise for her class's performance.

I might even get to sing a solo part or certainly be a main player in the class chorus. So when Ms. Marian asked for volunteers to sing a short solo for the concert, I was right there to show her what I could do. What came out of my mouth was not what I had heard in my brain. The class snickered and Ms. Marian said we needed to hear from other volunteers. Not the main part but certainly the chorus for me. But no, not the chorus either. "Who's off key?" 'It's Lynn.'

"Maybe you could play the tambourine. Everyone loves the Tambourine Man." "Sorry, you don't quite have the correct rhythm." I guess you have to know how to fit it into the music. I have never been accused of being able to Really Shake It. Maybe The Drum. Just beat the Drum. Oh my. You seem to have the upbeat and down-beat confused. Maybe that's why I still dislike "The Little Drummer Boy." Sometimes it is really hard to shake old memories. Triggers from the past can really disrupt current happiness. So I ended up playing a fake ukulele with yarn strings.

My music career was over. The word was out—Lynn DePeal can't carry a tune, he has no rhythm, and should never be included in anything musical.

Yet somewhere within me, the dream continued. I would overcome my musically-challenged self. I would keep trying. Even through the constant reminders of my family and friends that I just didn't have any musical aptitude. My sister played the piano and accordion. My brother got all kinds of accolades for his singing ability, he learned to play the guitar, and he could play the keyboard.

So I decided to try piano lessons. I got to the second piece in *Teaching Little Fingers to Play*. After six weeks with my teacher and not making progress on this challenging number, my parents decided not to let me continue. I was wasting my time and their money.

Outwardly, my musical dreams seemed to die. But not inside me, I still wanted to show everyone that I could do it. I tried secretly to play the trombone with the help of a friend. I couldn't quite stay on pitch and stay with the time of the beat. I tried the guitar and couldn't get my two hands coordinated. I stepped down to the ukulele (not the one with yarn strings-the real thing) but couldn't even tell if I had the simple "My Dog Has Fleas" tuning correct.

I tried the boy's glee club and found I could do all right if I just copied the guy next to me. But if I had to go on my own, I lost the tune in the chorus of other parts near me. I thought that I could possibly succeed if I could sing in a small group, memorize my part, and stick strictly to the lead part. A trio and a quartet later left me defeated again.

Down but not out. I even tried the piano again when I was in college, but once again, I got stuck on "The Song of the Volga Boatmen," the second piece in *Teaching Little Fingers to Play*. I was doomed to watch from the sidelines as everyone else joined in the celebration of music.

But time often brings new possibilities. Discarded dreams may rise up unannounced and new opportunities give promise to renewed faith. In my studies to be an elementary teacher, I had to take a required course in teaching music to elementary kids. With my history, I dreaded this class. I was sure that I would never make it through. I would be found out. I couldn't sing, move rhythmically, or even coordinate my feet to the beat. I would be humiliated in front of my teacher and classmates. But I made it. I not only loved the class, I learned something. I found that I not only loved music, I could enjoy it at a whole new level. I taught the class a very fun song: "I Am a Fine Musician." I saw it on *The Dick Van Dyke Show* and thought it would be a song that I could try in class. Dick, Sally, and Buddy made it the most fun song I had ever seen. I knew that I was the Mel of the group but what the heck. Give it a shot. I might die from embarrassment or at least be helped off the stage crying and humiliated. But that didn't happen. We had a ball performing that song. I was probably somewhat off-key and I'm sure I didn't get the beat just right. Certainly, my movements were a bit off, but we enjoyed every minute of it. The teacher and class cheered and clapped when we were done. I found the joy of music. Participation. Talent was not the key. I loved hearing it. I knew what sounded good to my ears. I might not always hit the right note but I could tell when others did. I couldn't perform the musical beat but I could feel when others did. I could tell that I had a musical brain. I could look at notes on a page and sing the song in my head. I could finally fully enjoy music on my own terms. I didn't have to be a great performer, although I still carry that fantasy with me. I could now enjoy all kinds of music and be certain what was good and what was bad. I was a self-ordained music editor. That might lead some of you to think I would become a music snob. Far from it. Because of my own lack of performing talent, I can look past the musical talent of the performers and feel the energy of the song or piece. I can appreciate the words and theme of the rendition. That's why I am so eclectic in my love for music. All kinds of music. From Chopin's *Études* to Carrie Underwood. From a Beethoven's symphony to Elvis Presley. From a Bach's concerto to the Eagles. From Josh Groban to Paul Revere & the Raiders. From Tony Bennett to Hank Williams Jr. From the Cathedral Quartet to Bob Seger. Just like the old the Oak Ridge Boys' tune, "She must have known the words to at least a million tunes," I have and an extremely long playlist. From this list, I have picked out three songs to be sung at my funeral. I would like them live, but I can't quite pin down the date. My wife says she could help me with that but I said a CD would be okay.

First, I want Ernie Haase singing "Oh, What a Savior." For those unfamiliar with him, Ernie sang the tenor part in the Cathedral Quartet, my favorite Southern gospel quartet of all time. Ernie now leads and manages a group called

Signature Sound. I love this song. It speaks truth and hope to me and I love Ernie's voice. I plan to sing with him in heaven.

Second, I want Bob Seger to perform "I Love That Old Time Rock and Roll." Can't you just feel the energy? Go ahead. Sing along. Come on, you disco fans, join in. You'll love it. I do, so I think everyone should. And when this song plays, I believe that I am actually a great dancer. I've got the moves. Just don't show me the videotape.

Finally, I want to have "Already Gone" by the Eagles. I can imagine everyone at the funeral standing and cheering as they sing, "Yes, I'm already gone … I will sing the vict'ry song." I'll be singing along with you as I look down from my heavenly place.

I sure hope Glenn Frey made his peace with God, because I want to hear him sing it again. And I'll join right in with him. I think my son feels the same way about the Foo Fighters. Not quite my style, but I sure wish he gets that opportunity.

I sure hope you are catching my excitement about music. I love to hear it and let it touch my ears and then my soul. But most of all, I love to participate. To participate doesn't always mean that I have to get up and sing the song or perform the piece. It means that I can be involved in the words, the rhythm, and the theme. My brain is actively processing what is being played or sung and I am a part of it. There is no better feeling. The blend of instruments, the harmony of voices, the emotion of a singer's heart, the interesting story, and the imaginative poetry of the verses.

Over the centuries, much of the greatest music has come out of the church. Poets and musicians have long offered sacrifices of praise to their God through Psalms and Hymns. From King David of the Bible through Bach and Handel, People have found that their praise was best offered through music. Martin Luther and Charles Wesley continued this tradition with some of the Best Loved Hymns of all time. The author of *It Is Well with My Soul* found peace in a time of tragedy by laying his soul before the God he loved. Henry Wadsworth Longfellow expressed his distress during the Civil War and then found comfort as he struggled with his poem "I Heard the Bells on Christmas Day." Black slaves created songs that have been labeled Negro spirituals as they struggled through the oppression of slavery.

The bluegrass music from the Appalachian Hills and the blues of Memphis are a part of this tapestry of music that came from and shaped the music of the church. Rock and roll had its origins in the Southern gospel of the country church and the old camp meeting days. Who can forget the early influences that church music had on Elvis Presley and Whitney Houston?

The history of church music is long and profound. The intermingling of the old and new. Different forms and different styles, but always a connection between the past and present. And always a common thread. The thread is participation. As I stated before, participation does not always involve a physical activity of being on stage performing. But it does require the engagement of the mind, the heart, the soul, and spirit. To really participate, the song and musicians must touch the part of man that reaches into the soul. Since the beginning of man, this connection has been called True Worship.

That brings me to my problem. Deep within me I have a craving to worship the God I love and serve through music. I would love to do that at church but I have found that in the past ten to fifteen years, I have found that it is increasingly difficult. Why is that so? I have concluded that it is because a whole new wave of Worship Leaders invaded the church music scene and have tossed away the beautiful bouquet of musical variety that has shaped the history of man's connection to God. They have locked away anything earlier than their own experience in a vault and are letting it be discarded or dismissed. Any mention of a song or style that they didn't create or embrace is tossed on the rubbish pile of the worn and useless. At best they reconfigure a song that has endured through time and has been embraced by generations of saints. The new worship team will take what is better and diminish it with their editing. What was, is old fashioned, boring, and has no place in the hip new church service.

I have been accused of being out of touch. I need to get with the program. No one listens to Southern gospel. The Gaithers are yesterday's news. Never heard of George Beverly Shea. Martin Luther has nothing to say to me. Fanny Crosby—didn't she sell candy?

So we have our worship team. Twenty minutes on Sunday morning, banging away on their drums and guitars, jumping around in their skinny jeans, and proclaiming that worship is really happening. Maybe if they opened their eyes and turned down the volume they would see that there is little participation and certainly no engagement. Their worship is an illusion. Led by those who wish they could perform on a bigger stage but lack the talent for it, we are saddled with worship leaders who I label wannabes. Those who would like to be on the big stage but don't have the talent to be there. No one would ever pay to listen to them perform. They are mediocre in their musical ability but consider themselves to be on the threshold of greatness. Their writing is trite and repetitious. Throw together a hodgepodge of platitudes and often an incoherent mix of thoughts and then repeat, repeat, repeat. Something is bound to stick. That's the plan. Toss in a bridge and we're done for the day. The performance is complete. Mission accomplished. We have really worshipped. Aren't we great? You couldn't manage without our leadership. One last guitar strum, a final beat of the drum, turn off the smoke, and fade the strobe lights. Our hearts and minds are now prepared for the sermon. I wish with all my being that this was true. Sadly, it is not.

I know that this is the contemporary church. You might ask why I go to a church like that. A good question.

It is because I really do love my church. I love the mission of the church I attend. The mission is to connect people first to God and then to other people. Spreading the Good News to those who are far from God. I love that mission. But the music, it is a distraction from true worship. It is a filler and has little connection to the one who created all of us. But it is only for fifteen to twenty minutes a week. I can put up with this noise for that short time and enjoy and worship in my own way the rest of the week. I am so thankful for Sirius Satellite Radio, CDs, and Pandora. My wife and I have created our own station and listen as we ready ourselves for Church. For those who haven't tried this venue, give a listen to David Phelps. You will think you are in heaven.

I want to think that heaven will be filled with all kinds of music. I read a book written by a man who said he had a glimpse of heaven when he died and then came back. He said that the music was beautiful. Described by the only word that fit, heavenly. I sure hope that what he saw is true. I want the music of heaven to be wonderful. After all, there should be no disappointments in heaven. But perhaps, I will have to live out eternity on the sidelines watching others perform the latest musical fad. It is possible that I will face my third heavenly disappointment.

Our Sunday morning praise band will be the worship leaders in heaven.

CHAPTER 4

I think I grew up poor, I didn't really know for sure. I was just like most of the other kids in my neighborhood. Two pairs of jeans, three or four Buster Brown T-shirts, a pair of tennis shoes, and some dress pants. Also a white shirt that I would wear to church. I often got these clothes as hand-me-downs from my older brother who was almost two years older than me. But he was always lots taller than me and I had to roll up the pant legs two or three turns so they didn't drag on the floor. I did get a new suit from Montgomery Ward's when I was eight. That was because my little brother died and Mom wanted me to look really nice at the funeral.

I did ask my Mom once when I was nine if we were poor. I told her that one of the kids at school said we were. She replied with, "You know, I guess we are." That was the last time I asked about that. I think my question made Mom feel bad and I didn't want to hurt her feelings.

But you know, I didn't feel poor. We were just like about everyone else in the neighborhood. We had food to eat, a warm house, a fun school (remember Ms. Marian), friends to play with, and imaginations that created every game we wanted to play. Cowboys and Indians. Simply find a string, tie a string around the head and put some bird feathers we found into the string. I was now an Indian. I could turn into a cowboy by nailing together a couple pieces of old wood and now I had a six shooter. We played army in an old discarded World War II tank left at the airport. We flew homemade kites made from willow branches, butcher paper, and flour paste. Tails for the kite were made from worn out shirts. My grandma taught us to make hook rugs out of rags. All the kids in the neighborhood came over to learn. I would shovel walks in the winter for a dime, rake leaves in the fall, and pull weeds in the summer. Since I lived in Traverse City, Michigan, I got to make big money in the summer by picking cherries with my Mom, I could make $10–15 in two weeks by picking cherries when I was eight and nine. I also got a nickel allowance each week for the chores I did at home. Doing the dishes each night with my older brother and sister. My brother always tried to get out of his share by faking a stomachache. He even tried to air-dry the dishes when it was his turn to dry them but my sister kept pouring water on them to make sure he did his part. I shoveled coal and chopped wood for our old Octopus Furnace, and carried out the wash water from our Kenmore Wringer Washer. All my money went to buy baseball cards except for a pair of ice skates that I bought for fifty cents from the Swap Shop. I traded up each year until I was eleven for a bigger pair. Just a trade in and twenty-five cents more. I lived on the ice rink in the winter and got to be second fastest ten-year old skater in Traverse City. But my love for baseball surpassed all other games and sports, and collecting major league baseball cards became an obsession. Topps packages for a nickel. Ten cards and a big stick of bubble gum, at least one pack every week. My goal was to collect each and every player, every year. I nearly did. I did get a lot of duplicates so lots of the boys traded with each other to complete sets. Some of the boys would even trade their cards for a stick of the gum. Great trade for me.

By the time I was thirteen, I had accumulated nearly three thousand cards. If I had known then what I know

now, there would have been no question as to whether I was rich. Just check the price of a Mickey Mantle rookie card in good condition. Not all of my cards were in good condition. My friends and I would put them in the spokes of our bike wheels to make a cool noise. Of course, my bike was a hand-me-down from my brother. It was too big for me. It only had one pedal, and it had a wobbly front wheel. But it was mine. We also used to line the cards up as teams and play a baseball game using a jackknife. Open up the small blade halfway and make it perpendicular to the ground. Open up the big blade so that it was horizontal to the ground. Stick the small blade in the ground and get your finger on the end of knife away from the big blade. Flip the knife in the air. If the big blade stuck in the ground with no other blades touching, home run. If the small blade stuck by itself, triple. If both blades stuck in the ground, double. If either blade stuck and the other blade touched the ground, single. If no blade stuck in the ground and the knife fell sideways, out.

We had regular season games using our cards and knife. We had all-star games. We had World Series games. We got to know every player on every team. I could usually tell you the current batting average of just about every major league baseball player. These guys were bigger than life to me. This was the 1950s. Baseball was the king of American sports. Players were heroes, and these heroes had no flaws. We knew nothing about the personal life of our idols. We weren't told of their womanizing, drunkenness, and racism. We lived in an idyllic time when all that mattered was the box score. Who hit one out of the park, who stole a base, and who could turn a double play. Which pitcher could throw the high hard one for a strikeout. What outfielder could stop a runner from going from first to third or scoring from second by firing the perfect strike to the base. Everyone had their team, and everyone had their player. For those in Saint Louis, it was probably Stan "the Man" Musial. For those on the north side of Chicago, it had to be Ernie Banks. In New York, Mickey Mantle almost made fans forget Babe Ruth and Joe DiMaggio. For me, living in Michigan, it was Al Kaline, number 6, youngest player to win the American League batting title at the age of twenty in 1955. Never played in the minor leagues, Mr. Detroit Tiger. Players seldom got traded then. I didn't understand it then and didn't care that players were really indentured servants. It never crossed my mind that a whole group of great players had not even been allowed to cross the racial barrier and play in the mostly white fraternity of Major League Baseball players. Those few black players that had crossed these lines were still a small minority in the national sport of a racially-divided country. I was an adult before I fully understood the discrimination that black athletes had faced during my innocent childhood. All I wanted was to grow up and play at Briggs Stadium (later renamed Tiger Stadium) and roam the expansive outfield of that storied place and share the glory with the player I wanted to emulate.

Growing up in Traverse City had insulated me from many of the realities of life. My school was a safe and friendly place. I never saw a teacher raise his hand or voice to a child. My neighborhood was just a group of kids getting along with each other. We lived together as a group that just wanted to get by and to get along.

The only minorities I saw were the migrant workers who came in the summer to pick the cherries and other fruit crops that were grown along the Lake Michigan shoreline. All I knew was going to school, attending church, doing my chores, ice skating in the winter, playing baseball in the summer, and cheering my tigers as I listened to them on the radio.

Things changed quite drastically when our family moved from Traverse City to the North End in Kalamazoo, Michigan. I didn't know it then but people referred to our area of the city as the bad part of town. I now attended a school with an even mixture of black, white, and Hispanic. The kids on our street were the same mix. I now saw teachers actually grab a hold of kids and give them a swat or a shake. I saw kids get into fights. I had known none of this. My only concern was to do well in school and find a group of kids who wanted to play a game of baseball and I found that. Kids like me. It didn't matter what color they were or what their primary language was, we were just kids looking for a game. A game that didn't cost much. A game that could be put together anyplace we could find an empty field. If someone could come up with some sort of a bat and small round ball, we could create a ballgame. My small backyard even became a ball field. Hitting select garage boards became singles, doubles, and triples and on the roof was a home run. Wrong board or over the roof was an out.

Out came the baseball cards and teams were formed. My favorite pastime continued.

My isolated, segregated life had changed and so was the game I loved. I still didn't know of behind-the-scenes cruelty that great players like Jackie Robinson, Hank Aaron, and Ernie Banks had to endure, but I got a close up view of the struggles of some of my neighborhood and baseball buddies. When one of my best friends was told by a white bully at church that, "Niggers weren't welcome here". I was shocked when the bully's dad jumped in to support his son. My Dad, who was the minister, showed me something that day by stepping in and telling the bully and his dad if they were going to treat someone like that, they should leave the church and never come back. It was a lesson that I never forgot.

It's inevitable that time moves us on to new places and events. Our circumstances change but we never lose all of the things that shaped us from our childhood.

My life's dream of being the next Al Kaline was lost due to a nagging sore arm, a weak bat, and fear that I would not succeed. So I quit baseball and moved in new directions. My blend of childhood friends scattered and took different paths. Our family moved to a new neighborhood and I huddled more closely to the groups that were more like me. My new high school friends, drawn more by academic success than athletic recognition led me away from those that just wanted a game. My church moved from the inner city to the suburbs. My place in the world was becoming defined.

I hung around with the best students but I was only good. I was 63 in a class of 625. My friends would go to the University of Michigan. I would settle for a little Christian college where there would be no chance of failure. My group got even smaller. I would marry the girl from my tiny church when she was eighteen and I was twenty. Neither of us had really examined who we were, what we wanted, and what we needed. We just took the easy and safe path that was right in front of us. No risks, no failure. But surprisingly, the road of no risks does lead to failure when the road comes to intersections or forks in the road. There is no safety then and we often stumble because the road of risk has never been attempted.

Along with changes in me, the world around was changing. Civil and racial unrest were rampaging through our country. College students were screaming in protest over a meaningless war and blacks were taking to the streets calling for justice and equal rights. I had this unsettled feeling that these calls for change were well founded, but I had been taught to believe in my government leaders and certainly the president. And I had grown up poor but was pulling myself up by my own initiatives. Why couldn't others do the same? So when the city of Detroit went up in flames in 1967, I was angry that those people would destroy this city where my beloved Tigers played. The neighborhoods near Tiger Stadium were burned and abandoned. It appeared that nothing could possibly heal this great divide.

But into this wasteland came a glimmer of hope: the 1968 Tigers. Forever a middle of the pack team, these Tigers with renewed passion and skill, forged their way to the front and brought a new sense of togetherness to that city. Whites and blacks had something in common. Their team, a mixed bag of various backgrounds, languages, and colors, made the statement that if we wanted to, we could get along and play the game together.

This recognition has shaped me forever. Baseball is the greatest analogy for life. Different than any other sport, it is a mixture of team and individual. No one player can do it alone but each player often stands on his own island and makes his personal contribution. The game moves at its own pace. There is no clock and each game has its own rhythm. There is very little to predict what will occur in the game. There is not a great deal of game planning. Just hand the ball to a pitcher, let the pitcher fire the ball to the plate and see if they can get the ball past the guy who wants to connect with that ball. Sometimes the batter wins, and sometimes the pitcher. All kinds of statistics are kept on this battle. Batting average, RBIs, On Base Percent (OBP), slugging percentage, ERA, WHIP, and on and on. Walks, runs, sacrifice bunt, game winning hits, hits with men in scoring position, Strikeouts (swinging or Called). The list is seemingly endless.

Football and basketball are team games. An individual player can make an impact but they can't control the game. A player is only as good as his team. Golf is determined solely by the performance of the individual. Baseball is the only game that truly emulates life.

So my love for baseball was renewed. I had lost interest in the game and had even thrown away my baseball cards because they got a little mildewed in the closet and I was tired of moving them from house to house. I should have seen the future and taken better care of them. They would be worth a fortune today.

Yet, in September of 1968, I took my pregnant wife to see the World Series bound Detroit Tigers. I had gotten the tickets in July and had no idea that Denny McClain would be pitching for his thirtieth win. But there we were in the Upper Deck, just off the backstop screen, behind the TV broadcast booth. Dizzy Dean, the last thirty game winner, and two former Dodger Greats Pee Wee Reese, and Sandy Koufax, were announcing the game. They all had to walk by me to get to the booth and Sandy Koufax stopped to sign autographs. He didn't get to me but he put his hand on my shoulder to steady himself. I haven't washed that shirt since. Pee Wee was very friendly to everyone but Dizzy Dean just walked right on by.

I will never forget that day. John Donaldson of the Oakland Athletics hit a foul ball off Denny McClain. The ball went up on the screen and instead of rolling back on the field as usual it rolled off the side. I saw it coming my way, leaped up, and got the ball amidst ten other hands.

What a thrill! The Tigers came back to win that game 5–4 and Denny McClain won his thirtieth. I tried to get on the field for a signature on the ball but the mob around McClain kept me from doing that. We took a picture of my pregnant wife outside Tiger Stadium holding that ball.

Our son was born in January 1969. He grew up loving baseball. Just like me. He loved to play catch with me. I knew he was destined to be a great player. I tucked the prized ball away in a safe place in a closet. I got it out periodically to show friends but eventually the story got old and I kind of forgot about the ball.

Five years later, we moved from that house and I went to the closet to retrieve the souvenir. It was gone. Where was it? Nobody knew. Evidently someone had come into our house and bypassed all our other valuables and stole that unsigned ball.

Five more years passed and my son, now ten, came to me and confessed. "Remember that ball from the closet? I took it out and played catch with my friend and lost it down the hill toward the lake. I was afraid to tell you because I thought you would be mad." I was a little miffed when I heard this confession, and maybe I would have been furious back then, but my son was more important than a ball. Furthermore, it would be a good story and an old memory just like my baseball cards.

Years later, after my son was married and he was expecting his first child, I was retelling the story of the McClain ball to a friend at work. A week later he came to work with a baseball signed by Denny McClain. How did that happen?

After I had told him the story, he thought it was such a good one that he told his neighbor in Holland, Michigan. It just so happened that his neighbor's Dad worked for radio in Detroit. She told her Dad who then passed it on to Denny McClain who sometimes worked for WJR too, thus the signed ball. I presented that new ball to my new grandson with a Denny McClain 1968 baseball card and a picture of my pregnant wife outside the stadium. I hope no one plays with that ball and loses it.

My son never got to the major leagues. I'm not sure if it was a lack of talent or just a lack of determination but he did provide me with an avenue to coach the game I loved. Little League was always looking for coaches, so when the opportunity came up, I jumped in. I got to help coach my son and enjoy his accomplishments. From no-hit pitching to game- winning home runs.

I coached for ten more years after my son had moved on from Little League. I loved it. Baseball was my world. From coaching the team to watching the other teams in the area. Learning, teaching the game, and keeping stats. Fully understanding what baseball meant in the life of a young man. Baseball taught life. It taught young men how to stand up to a demanding situation and not back down. Imagine a ten-year-old standing in the batter's box and facing a dominant twelve-year-old pitcher. Shaking at the knees and learning to stand in there and take his swings. Success is not about getting a hit, but making the attempt. Taking a risk of failure and maybe putting the ball in play. Not just standing there and getting called out, but moving out of the safety zone and getting into the game. Every boy needs this experience. I had often avoided those risk taking moments in my life but I would now help other boys to do it. I would encourage them to take their cuts. Do your best and don't measure your success by your high percentage of hits. Even the greatest players only got on base 40 percent of the time. That's even counting walks and errors.

So I had a lot to say about how baseball was the best life lesson of all. Nothing was better for a boy than to learn the lessons of personal risk and the togetherness of team play. Not all boys were created with equal talent, but hard work and determination meant something, and boys need to push themselves to the highest level of performance that was within them. And then it is important to join a team and work toward common goals. Not everyone was equal, but everyone should have equal opportunity. Physique, size, speed, background, color, or language were not important, desire and perseverance were the key. That is what life should be.

Yet, around this time there was a movement in our society. People were getting equality and equal opportunity confused. This was showing up in our schools, jobs, and politics. Everyone should be treated the same, be given the same playing time, and share in the same rewards. Performance didn't matter, everyone should participate in the same way and be given the same participation trophy. Grades in school should be eliminated, and affirmative action should be instituted so that everyone could join whether they earned it or not. Equal pay based on showing up and not based on production. Such was the new social and political environment, and baseball was affected. Every child should play and have equal time on the field. Every child should bat in rotation whether he's on the field or not. Everyone plays and everyone sits out the same amount. No strikeouts. Just keep batting until the ball goes in play. Cheer for everything, don't even keep score, it's bad for self-esteem. Present everyone a trophy for participating.

But Little League Baseball was not changing fast enough for some. This group created their own recreation leagues where these new rules could take immediate effect. They make loud noises against the Little League that still cared about winning and made some separations between good play and bad. The cry was that these folks loved the kids more and didn't want them to feel bad.

In the midst of this change came a new phenomenon in the United States. An old game was imported from Latin America and Europe but with slightly different rules. The game was as my grandson Mason would say, "Exactly the same—Just a little different." Yes, they had the same ball, the same gear, the same players, and the same idea of moving the ball downfield with the feet, body, and head (no hands) and kicking the ball in the net past the one standing in front of the goal. That game was soccer. Unlike the Latin American and European version of the game, this Americanized soccer, tossed away the highly competitive nature of the game and introduced the rules that supporters had challenged in baseball. The intense competitiveness of the real soccer game that often brought violence and riots to the fans and players was exchanged for the new American thought process.

Everyone plays, talent and performance didn't matter. Trophies are for everyone and no need to keep score. Tell that to a soccer kid from Mexico, France, or Brazil and you would have a riot on your hands.

American kids would hop in their Mom's minivan and be escorted to the newly created fields. Dressed in their brand new shoes, socks, and protective knee, ankle, and elbow pads, all the kids would run around and participate in this wonderful form of exercise. There were always two or three kids that didn't quite get the concept. They actually thought it was important to keep score and keep track of the number of goals that they personally scored. Shame on you kids for being rebels to the cause. You competitive kids missed the point. This is not about learning the game, improving yourself, and attempting to move to a higher level.

This game is about self-esteem, inclusiveness, and the rejection of the competitive nature of baseball.

I blame the demise of this country on minivans. That is because minivans represent everything that is wrong with this country. These minivans driven by soccer moms take their coddled children to these fields of play, and praise them for non-existent achievements. And since the kids are more than an arm's length away from the parent, they have no fear of a father's hand coming back and grabbing them to correct bad behavior. Shouldn't every child experience Dad's hand coming back on the knee with a threat to stop the car.

Just like every movement, the knee jerk reaction of misguided groups ends when their movement is threatened by the real world. American soccer is now joining the game that has been going on in the rest of the world for many years. Soccer teams created just for play are being replaced by teams that actually want to compete. Skill and talent are rewarded. There are efforts to make sure children have

the instruction and training to put them in a place to succeed. Performance does matter. The score counts. Soccer in
America is becoming what the rest of the world has known
for a long time. Trophies are earned, not given.

But the introduction of soccer in this country left a bad
taste in my mouth. I can't overcome the distaste I feel when
someone commends soccer to me. I can't get excited when
France beats Germany one-nil in a championship match.
The names Eduardo, Felipe, and Pelé just don't make my
heart beat faster like the Babe, Mickey, Hammering Hank,
and Mr. October.

So when I get to heaven and find that soccer is the
national sport of heaven, I will experience my fourth greatest disappointment.

CHAPTER 5

Sometimes, my mind takes off on a journey in which I have no destination. But I think you already know that about me. All of a sudden, a word or phrase mentioned by someone near me will send me on one of these trips. I could be standing right next to you and actually be far away in a distant seemingly forgotten place that has been resurrected in my memory reservoir. Sometimes that journey comes in the form of a dream. Not deep REM sleep dreaming. Active, as real as it gets, dreams. Conversational, argumentative, kicking away snake dreams. I have no idea what triggers these thoughts but they come frequently. My doctor says I need to have a sleep evaluation but I know that doctor will say I have sleep apnea and will need a CPAP machine. Has a sleep disorder doctor ever prescribed anything else? I probably need a psychiatrist instead but why fork out big dollars to find out something

I already know? I've got trails in my brain that can never be removed. The trails may be old and brushed covered, but they are permanently imbedded in the far recesses of my mind. Besides, my dreams are quite interesting, and even though they confuse my wife and often wake her in the night, they often provide a rather bizarre but stimulating story line.

Recently I dreamed about a kid named Milton Dodge. Milton was nine when I was five living in Detroit, Michigan. Detroit of 1950 was different than the Detroit we know today. Inside 8 Mile, there were working-class neighborhoods occupied by those who worked in or supported the auto industry. Everyone knew everyone else in the neighborhood. There were a lot of open spaces with small woods, ponds, and fields. All of the kids with great imaginations would play together in these places.

Every neighborhood always has one kid that none of the parents want their children to play with. Not necessarily because the child is so bad, but because he is just too wild, just too impulsive, and unpredictable. He was the kid that would lead all the other kids into some kind of trouble. Milton Dodge was that kid. For the very reasons that the parents warned us to stay away from Milton, the rest us of were drawn to him as a human magnet.

Milton was always discovering something new. He was always on a new adventure. Milton wasn't afraid of anything. Not only did Milton have a Swiss Army knife, he carried a hatchet. Just think of the possibilities.

With Milton, we kids chopped down small trees and built forts. We dug holes in the woods and tried to trick the timid neighborhood wuss to fall in the covered hole. Milton would dare us to walk across the newly frozen ponds to see if we had the courage to continue even when the ice cracked around us. No matter that the ponds were only eighteen inches deep. Milton taught us to be brave.

As I look back, I think Milton was a reincarnation of John the Baptist. An untamed boy crying in the wilderness eating locusts and wild honey. He would get us to sample ants, tell us that worms tasted good, even gulped down tadpoles that we caught in the ponds. He informed us that these tadpoles would grow into frogs and frog legs tasted great. I never did develop an appetite for these exotic foods but I did give them all a try. Not always willingly, but Milton had a way about him. Either taste these awesome delicacies or have them rammed down your throat. It was better to do your own taste test.

I know that many of you may be wondering how a story of sixty-five years ago about a boy named Milton Dodge could possibly have anything to do with the book you are reading. But of course, you should know that there is a connection. There is always a connection. You might not see the connection immediately and possibly many of you will walk away later and still not get it. But to me, it makes perfect sense.

When I was in third grade, I had to go live with my grandmother and old maid aunt because my parents spent a lot of their time with my dying little brother who was in Harper Hospital in Detroit. I actually lived with them for a total of three months before my brother died. My grandmother used to pick dandelion greens, boil them in an iron pot until they were mushy and serve them as the vegetable of the day. She said they were good for you but I suspect the real reason for serving them was because they didn't cost anything and they were plentiful. My grandmother was a product of the great depression and she didn't waste anything. She made her own lye soap, had a big garden and raised her own chickens. As I mentioned before, she taught me and all of the neighborhood kids how to make hook rugs out of old rags. Because she never tossed anything, her house was quite messy but I loved my grandma because she made me feel important and needed. I would gather eggs from the hen house, count the money that she made from selling some of those eggs, and help care for the garden as I watched it grow.

I don't think that my grandmother was a very good cook, but what did I know. My mother had learned from her so my diet didn't change much when I went to live with my grandmother. She cooked what she could afford, from the food she could gather from nature to the produce she could grow in her garden. From the chickens she could raise, to the free scraps or low-cost cuts of the butcher shop. I had to eat what was set before me. My dad had made that clear when I made a face at the dinner table once and mumbled that what I had been given tasted like puke. My dad grabbed me by the arm, escorted me out of the dining room, and made it clear that I was never to complain about the food my mom put in front of me. My mom did the best she could with what she had. So politely say thank you and enjoy what you get.

So the food fare, and the food I would get through all my growing up years would be very simple. Potatoes grown from the garden, always boiled, then sliced or mashed. Carrots, green beans, turnips, beets, and corn all boiled in an iron pot until they were almost soup. Keep the lid tight to keep in the vitamins. Picnic ham on Sunday. Leftover pieces in scalloped potatoes, ham bone with some meat attached for bean or pea soup. Don't waste anything. Sometimes the cheapest cut of beef roast on Sunday, saved by the butcher for my mom because no one else wanted it. Leftovers on Monday of roast beef and gravy on bread and then the scraps mixed with homemade noodles on Tuesday. Toss in liver and onions somewhere in the week followed by the old standby chip beef on toast. I think that was the food that got me escorted out of the room by my Dad. When funds ran real short, we got creamed corn on bread or chopped up bread in milk. Those had been staples of my parents growing up in the Depression. Any small complaints about our lack of variety of food would lead to a dissertation of what it was like growing up in the expression or a commentary on "the kids in China would be thankful for what you have." We never went to a restaurant and I had no idea of what a steak tasted like.

I can't say that I developed a keen palate in regard to food as I was growing up. I didn't have enough experience to know what I would really enjoy. I just knew some of the things I had come to hate and vowed that when I was older, I would never put them in my mouth again. I had quite a list. I wouldn't eat ants, worms, or tadpoles offered by Milton. Nor would I ingest dandelion greens, rhubarb, parsnip, beets, boiled carrots, lima beans, mince pie, and liver with onions. If it wasn't the texture, it was the look or smell that would make me puke. My dad couldn't stop me from saying puke now.

Somehow we think that when we are away from parental control, we will cast off everything we disliked about our childhood. But that is seldom the case. We can't quite get away from our early environment or the genetics that are forever with us. We may think we can move away and become a new person or totally recreate ourselves into someone new. But as the book written by Jon Kabat-Zinn says, "Wherever you go, there you are."

So adulthood brought immediate subtraction to my diet. No more hated boiled vegetables, no more liver, and no ruining strawberry pie with rhubarb. I would never touch bread and milk together again. I could eat what I wanted (sort of.) But I got married young and now I had to deal with a wife who brought her own culinary history into the mix. Homemade pizza, sloppy joes, potato pancakes, chili, spaghetti, and shepherd's pie. New possibilities were opening up. A roast beef or ham was still a staple on Sunday, but now it was an English cut with carrots cooked with beef consommé in the roast pan. And the ham would be an Armor Gold Star, not a Red Star. Gold Star all the way. I was on my way upward. We even had a steak once in a while but we really knew nothing about medium rare or the perfect temperature on a grill.

With some improved finances, we even got to eat out from time to time. Bill Knapp's, the Sveden House, Holly's Steak and 4, Sizzler, and Ponderosa. A new world of culinary delight with the coming of Chi Chi's, we opened up a brand new exotic possibility. Mexico brought to Grand Rapids, Michigan. Free chips and salsa, free refills on soda, and a Brand new taste. I could hear Milton Dodge saying, "Go for it."

Now my children would expand their food choices far beyond the choices of my youth. They had opportunities that I had never known existed. But they still needed to eat their vegetables. They had important vitamins and minerals that were essential to good health. But my daughters were not eager participants in eating what we had been taught were good for them. I wasn't going to force those overcooked carrots, beets, and peas on them. Nor would I force them to eat the dreaded lima beans but they certainly should taste broccoli or asparagus cooked by a newly discovered method of cooking vegetables—steaming. That was it, not mushy anymore. Delicious. Touch them up with a hollandaise sauce. My oldest daughter would reluctantly sample and sometimes enjoy the choices made for her but her younger by three minutes sister refused. She would clamp her mouth and shut with no possibility of hated foods entering her system. She would die of starvation before she would eat anything she didn't like. I tried a few times with some suggested methods and decided I would let her eat whatever she wanted.

I know that the food choices that my children grew up with are either enjoyed today because of the fond memories of the taste of our table fare or have been totally discarded because certain foods remind them of puke. You know the apple doesn't fall far from the tree. My kids will never eat Franco American spaghetti with Velveeta, ground beef, and onions again. I think I have ruined any possibility that they would try venison or microwaved chicken smothered in marinara sauce. They can make their own way now and deal with their own children.

But one thing our family still has in common is that we love food. Not all the same foods, although we do have some old family favorites. I did get remarried so I no longer have to tell my wife that her shepherd's pie was delicious. I did have to taste a whole new batch of Dutch and Swedish recipes that my new wife Nancy brought to the relationship. She inherited them or created them from her different family background. Her mom always made a couple of family favorites when we came to her house for dinner. Chicken piccata and coconut cream pie. Somehow My new mother-in-law had gotten the idea that I loved these dishes. She never knew to the day she died that these were two of my least favorite foods. I guess my Dad's lesson was imbedded in me forever. I simply ate the prepared meal and with a smile said "Thank you. It was great."

She never knew that I am a red meat guy. Grill it, roast it, season and cook. Add a simple salad with lettuce, tomatoes, cucumbers, and cheese and I'm good to go. Don't ruin anything with ingredients I can't pronounce.

I can say with certainty that our family, even with our likes and dislikes, are not skinny people. We love food. We think about food. We devour food. Even while we are eating a meal, we are thinking about the next one. All-inclusive resorts can be a real problem. Huge amounts of food with not enough time to eat it, what a dilemma. Just thinking of a medium rare New York strip grilled to perfection on a perfect temperature grill makes me moan with anticipation. It is almost better than sex. Note that I said almost. Driving into Carrabba's in Atlanta on our annual trip to Florida, preparing to order a sirloin Marsala creates a feeling of anticipation that is greater than my childhood Christmas Morning. My son is in search of the greatest prime-rib sandwich in the United States. Right now, it is Knight's Restaurant in Dexter, Michigan. We stopped there after a University of Michigan football game. We had met the owners of Knight's waiting in line for breakfast at a favorite Chicago eatery. One of my favorites, The West

Egg. They told us to stop by their restaurant in Dexter. We did, and they were right about the great food. My son is also a connoisseur of wings. He lived in Buffalo, New York, and has tasted the best. So don't call them chicken wings or Buffalo wings, or you won't be allowed to recommend your favorite wing joint. They are, as all true wing lovers know, simply wings.

My step daughter and her husband are real foodies. They are always on a mission to discover the new greatest taste. They often share this search for the ultimate taste with their good friends, Steve and Michelle Oakley. Steve is a renowned chef in Indianapolis where he owns his own restaurant. Wouldn't you know it, he calls it Oakley's. He gets a lot of recognition for his food preparation. He even beat Bobby Flay on the Food Channel. The four of them often check out new eating places to see if they measure up. They all love food, think food, and inhale food.

As I get older, I have found that change does not come as easily as it once did. It is more comfortable to stay in the familiar and the known. From the simplicity of having Ma Bell take care of our telephone needs to shopping at the neighborhood supermarket. I now need an electrical engineering degree to pick out the correct light bulb. We can no longer just grab the Spic and Span to clean our floors and counters. We have to determine if its quartz, granite, marble, Formica, ceramic tile, or some form of fabricated material. We are bombarded with information and choices. Most of them make the older generation want to just throw up our hands and let the young ones sort it all out, and they are perfectly willing to do it. When my five-year-old grandson heard me complaining that this new program on my computer was really hard, he told me clearly, "Grandpa, it's not hard, it may be challenging for you but it's not hard."

Probably one of the greatest areas of choice and change has come in the food industry. You have seen some of the choices I have experienced in my lifetime and the choices my kids have experienced. I thought the increase in options that I have seen were quite dramatic but they are nothing compared to what is going on now. Somehow, in the current discussion and presentation of food, I think that the food industry is being taken over by a group a people who really dislike food. They write about food, they talk about food, they dominate the food industry with their pronouncements and recipes. But it is obvious that the don't understand a real love affair. They never mention the mouthwatering taste of a perfectly grilled steak. Eating veal is not ethical. It is cruel to ever bring wild game to the table. What you eat becomes a political statement. They are more concerned about the anti-oxidant value of a dish than the taste. They rate the quality of the food by its nutritional value and the numeric count of vitamins rather than savor the aroma and pure delight that comes from the meal. They have created terms and definitions that do not touch my gastronomical interest but appeal to the millennials. Terms like free radical scavengers, mocktails, zoodles, healthy flammatory response, nutrient dense, jícama, and daikon have replaced the only response to a meal, which is, "Man, that tasted good. Probably the best I ever had." Nothing portrays this shift better than two foods that have become popular in the past several years, quinoa and kale. Quinoa is a seed that even the birds won't eat. It is coated with saponin and is terribly bitter. Proponents can't possibly like it since they are constantly promoting its nutritional value and forever letting everyone know how to cook or combine it to get the bitter taste from our mouths. Kale is a leaf cabbage and is proclaimed by the new food experts to be an essential source of many of the nutritional ingredients that the body needs. It is deemed a miracle food which has huge benefits to the body's systems. All of this promotion is to cover the fact that the taste of kale is revolting. Somewhere between dirt and an old newspaper. Furthermore, it is fibrous and chewy if not prepared exactly as instructed. I am convinced that it is the main menu item for the anorexic, bulimic foodies that often visit the morning information shows. I say, "If you're going to barf it up anyway, it tastes the same coming up as it did going down."

So my dream of Milton Dodge made me think of all the things he tried to get me to eat. That led to thinking of my childhood food choices, which naturally led to my personal evolution of food likes and dislikes. Of course that would lead to my children and how they have carried on the traditions of eating. I now have grandchildren and they are right in the midst of a changing world. Food is right in the middle of that changing world. I hope this helps you understand the natural and clear thought process that brought us to this point. And this brings me to my final great concern. When I die and look forward to a great heavenly feast, I hope I will not face a terrible disappointment. My hope is that the chief chef of heaven is not a vegetarian or one of the new food mafia as many of today's generation wish. If that is heaven, I will be crushed.

CONCLUSION

When the idea for this book originated in my mind, I had thought I would come up with ten disappointments in heaven. But as I began to write, I found that I was beginning to stretch a bit when I got past the five I included. Besides, I realized that I could probably offend 90–95 percent of the population with the ones that I have chosen. Reaching the remaining minority would take a lot more effort than I wished to undertake. So if none of my disappointments offended you in any way, you are either just like me (which would be hard to imagine), or you just don't really care about anything. I just may include you in the sequel. I would hate to share heaven with those of you who stand for nothing.

There were a few topics that didn't make the list. My wife said they were too obscure or too personal. Especially the one of finding that my ex-wife had the mansion next to mine. I was told to keep that one out of the book. So I didn't bring it up. And you know how concerned I am about not hurting anyone's feelings.

So there you have it. Hope you enjoyed my ramblings. I certainly enjoyed writing the book. You may have learned something about how my mind works, and I had a great time traveling down some old paths. Just don't be mad at me and hold a long grudge. Believe me, holding grudges is not healthy.

ABOUT THE AUTHOR

Lynn is a retired door and hardware consultant living in Indianapolis, Indiana, with his wife, Nancy. He was born into a preacher family and heard early and often what heaven would be like. Now seventy years later, he decided to clear up some of the confusion by offering some possible alternatives to the more common conceptions. This is his first attempt at putting these musings to print. When not thinking contrary positions, Lynn loves to fish, read, and spend the winter in Naples, Florida.

CPSIA information can be obtained
at www.ICGtesting.com
Printed in the USA
FSHW01n1624221018
53072FS